DESERT ANIMALS AT NIGHT

DESERT ANIMALS

Rourke Publications, Inc.
Vero Beach, Florida 32964

© 1997 Rourke Publications, Inc.

Edited by Pamela J.P. Schroeder

PHOTO CREDITS
Photos p. 7, 10, 12, 15, 17, 18 © Joe McDonald; p. 4, 8, 13, 21,
title page, and cover © Lynn M. Stone

ACKNOWLEDGEMENT
The author thanks the staff of the Arizona-Sonora Desert Museum,
Tucson, for its cooperation with some of the photography in
this book.

Library of Congress Cataloging-in-Publication Data
Stone, Lynn M.
   Desert animals at night / by Lynn Stone.
      p. cm. — (Desert animals)
   Summary: Describes the behavior of desert animals that are
active at night, including bats, owls, foxes, and toads.
   ISBN 0-86625-626-1
   1. Nocturnal animals—Juvenile literature. 2. Desert animals—
Juvenile literature. [1. Nocturnal animals. 2. Desert animals.]
I. Title. II. Series: Stone, Lynn M. Desert animals.
QL755.5.S895   1997
591.754—dc21   97-16379
                                                      CIP
                                                       AC

Printed in the USA

TABLE OF CONTENTS

THE DESERT AT NIGHT

With the coolness of desert nights, animals begin to stir. The moonlight makes shadows of animals flying, running, walking, crawling, and just waiting.

Desert days during the warm months can be very hot. Most desert animals hide in burrows under sand or rocks. The sun and heat can kill.

By **dusk** (DUSK), when the sun sets, the desert cools rapidly. For desert animals, it is time to hunt—and be hunted.

For the mountain lion and other predators of the desert, the coolness of night is hunting time.

BATS

Bats are common on America's deserts, but they're not often seen. Bats are **nocturnal** (nahk TUR null), active at night.

During the day, bats hide in caves, buildings, and old mine tunnels. At night, these amazing flying **mammals** (MA muhlz) catch insects on the wing.

Bats hunt with **echolocation** (eh koh loh KAY shun). When their squeaks hit an object—even as small as an insect—they echo back to the bat. From the echo, a bat can tell if it has found prey or a rock.

The western pipistrel bat of southwestern deserts is usually the first bat to leave its perch and fly at night.

OWLS

Owls patrol the desert skies at night, too, taking over for the daytime hunting hawks.

These **predators** (PRED uh torz) hunt rats, mice, snakes, and even skunks. The smallest owls, such as the elf, hunt large insects and spiders.

Owls have good tools for night hunting. They have sharp toenails called **talons** (TA lunz). They also have special eyes for night vision.

Owls have great hearing. Even the noise of a mouse feeding on seeds can catch an owl's ears.

Keen eyes and ears keep the desert great horned owl's night flights on target.

FOXES

Foxes see fine at night, but they depend more on their noses and ears to find prey.

Foxes, both kit and desert grays, hide out in dens by day. At night they prowl the desert for rodents, like kangaroo rats. They also catch birds and eat some plant material.

The kit fox is a light-colored, big-eared animal. Like an owl, it can target its prey by sound.

The gray fox is the only North American fox that can climb trees.

Working nights is a way of life for the gray fox, who hides out by day.

CATS

Bobcats and mountain lions are common in North America. Some of them live in the deserts, or nearby. North of Mexico, the mountain lion is the largest of the wild cats. It may weigh 150 pounds (68 kilograms) or more.

Like other furry predators, these wild cats hunt mostly at night. Cats have excellent night vision and hearing.

Mountain lions will kill almost any animal. Mostly, they prey on deer and the piglike peccary, or javelina (hah vel EE nuh). Bobcats kill young deer, but they live mostly on birds and other small prey.

The desert bobcat has excellent night vision and sharp hearing, making it a successful predator at night.

TOADS

The desert is not the best place for frogs and toads. **Amphibians** (am FIB ee enz) like moisture, and deserts are dry.

Spadefoot toads, however, like the desert. They can bury themselves in soil for a long time—and live. They use a spade-shaped "toe" on each hind foot to dig.

Spadefoots crawl out when rain hits the desert, which isn't often. They call loudly to attract mates. Spadefoots lay eggs in rain pools.

Lit by a camera's flash, a spadefoot toad calls for a mate after an evening thunderstorm on the desert.

SCORPIONS

Many **species** (SPEE sheez) of scorpions and their tarantula cousins live in the American deserts. The largest of the scorpions is the giant desert scorpion. It has a 5 1/2-inch (14-cm) long body!

Scorpions hunt insects, spiders, and other small, boneless animals. Scorpions have a stinger at the tip of their "tail." They kill most of their prey, however, by biting, not stinging.

The only scorpion that is dangerous to people is the sculptured scorpion of Arizona.

A giant desert hairy scorpion, seen in a camera's flash, hunts in Arizona's Saguaro National Park.

SNAKES

Snakes can die easily in the desert's summer heat. Most snakes stay out of the sun and hunt at night.

The night snake of the deserts is well-named. People don't see it often, and then only at night. Night snakes hunt lizards and insects. They kill with a poisonous bite.

The night snake's bite can't hurt a person. The rattlesnake's can.

Several species, or kinds, of rattlesnakes live in the Southwestern deserts. They, too, are nocturnal hunters, looking for rabbits and rodents.

Rarely seen because of its nocturnal habits, a night snake is "caught" by a camera's flash on the Sonoran Desert.

RODENTS

Rodents are mammals with special teeth for gnawing. The desert has many kinds of rodents—rats, mice, ground squirrels, gophers, and porcupines.

Rodents live largely by eating plant parts. They're important prey for desert predators, like badgers, foxes, coyotes, snakes, bobcats, owls, and hawks.

One of the most interesting desert rodents is the kangaroo rat. Its 8-inch (20.5-cm) tail balances its 6-inch (15.4-cm) body as it jumps like a kangaroo.

Glossary

amphibian (am FIB ee en) — the group of soft, cold-blooded, air-breathing animals with backbones and smooth, moist skin; toads, frogs, salamanders, and kin

dusk (DUSK) — the period of last light after sunset and before darkness

echolocation (eh koh loh KAY shun) — a system of echo-making squeaks used by bats to find prey and other objects in their flight path

mammal (MA muhl) — the group of air-breathing, warm-blooded, milk-producing animals with hair, or fur, and a backbone

nocturnal (nahk TUR null) — active at night

predator (PRED uh tor) — an animal that kills other animals for food

species (SPEE sheez) — a certain kind of animal within a closely-related group of animals; for example, a *spadefoot* toad

talon (TA lun) — the clawed toes of birds of prey (owls, hawks, eagles)

INDEX